MW01153392

A Tree for Me

Copyright © 2020 Stephanie Lindabury MacKendree
All rights reserved
First Edition

Fulton Books, Inc.
Meadville, PA

Published by Fulton Books 2020

ISBN 978-1-64654-357-1 (hardcover)
ISBN 978-1-64654-358-8 (digital)

Printed in the United States of America

A Tree for Me

Stephanie Lindabury MacKendree

Every year, my family and me
Drive to the farm to cut down our tree.

We hop in the car for the long, long drive
And count all the Christmas trees passing by.

I count on my fingers again and again
While my little sister counts ten by ten.

Our goal is to count one hundred trees
So we can high-five and shout yippee!

Our favorite part is the tractor ride,
Even when it's cold outside.

Now it's time to find our tree
We all follow Daddy while we look and see.

The tree we want should be taller than him,
wide enough to hug, but not too thin.

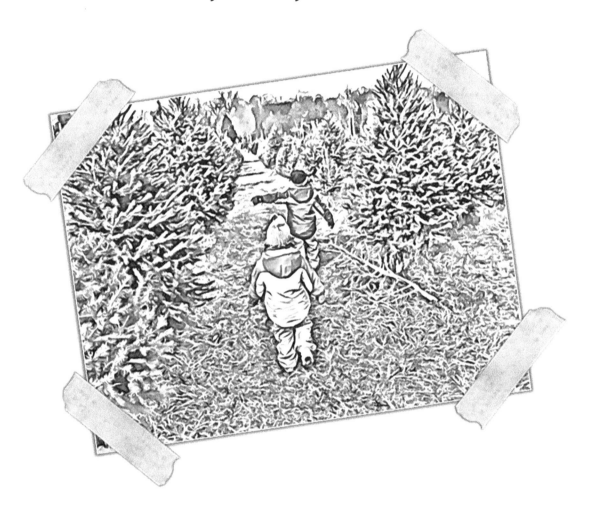

Is this our tree?

No, too round.

Is this our tree?

No, too dry and too brown.

Is this our tree?

No, it's just too small.

— 2 feet —

Is this our tree?

No, that's much too tall.

10 feet

70 to 100 feet

New York City's Rockefeller Plaza has the tallest tree of all.

Is this our tree?

No, that's way too wide, and

yikes! There's an animal living inside!

It can't be too pointy,
too crooked,
or thick.
Sharp needles might give your finger a prick.

Ouch!

Is this our tree?

No, too big for the car.

Is this our tree?

No, that's too far.

Will we ever find our tree?

Maybe there is no tree for me.

Wait, what's this I see?

This tree is just right for me!

Not too pointy, dry, or wide.
There are no animals living inside.

Not too crooked and not too thick.
Not too big or too far to pick.

Not too round and not too small.
Not too brown and not too tall.

I help cut it down and watch it fall.

This tree is definitely the best tree of all!

We keep a slice of the bottom each year
To create a special keepsake and memories so dear.

Now after fourteen years, it is only mom, sis, and me

And I am the one who cuts down the tree.

Our friends are like family, so we invite them along

To make new memories and keep our traditions strong.

There will always be a tree for me.

You'll find one too, just look and see.

About the Author

Stephanie Lindabury MacKendree was inspired to write *A Tree for Me* by her children, Drew and Cate, as she followed them through the tree farm, searching for the perfect Christmas tree. Cutting down their own tree is a tradition they started in 2006 after moving to Larchmont, New York, from Manhattan. It remains an annual favorite holiday activity although their family structure has changed. After writing the initial story, Stephanie partnered with her brother, David Lindabury, to finish the manuscript. Together they are bringing it to life.

The tradition of saving the Christmas tree bottom was started by their parents, Paula and Steve Lindabury. They recently gave each of their children the tree bottom from the year they were born.

This year start the tradition in your house. Simply cut a slice from the bottom when you purchase your tree or before you put it in water. Write the year on the bottom and begin your collection. Turn it into an ornament or other holiday keepsake. They create a lasting and one-of-a-kind way to cherish your family's most special holiday memories. Share your collection with us at Treesandmemories.com.

CPSIA information can be obtained
at www.ICGtesting.com
Printed in the USA
LVHW070844131020
668669LV00024B/1385